elga antonsen
road dance

poems

elga antonsen

road dance

poems

SOUL GARDEN PRESS

MALDEN-ON-HUDSON, NEW YORK

"Muscadine" and an early version of "Saturn's Return," SUNY New Paltz, *Women's Studies Newsletter,* 1984.

"Daisy Chains" and "Light Travel at Twenty" first published in *The Woodstock Seasoner,* Autumn 1984.

Published in the United States by:
Soul Garden Press, P. O. Box 49, Malden-on-Hudson, NY 12453
Cover Design: Davis Design Company, New York City

Antonsen, Elga
    Road Dance
    ISBN: 978-0-615-36205-2
    1. Poetry 2. Hudson Valley 3. Environmentalism

DEDICATION

*To Ruth Carr Brown Laurence (2/14/1918-
2/20/2008) whose gifts make this book possible.*

*Ruth fostered the careers of those she trained in
the workplace, and in retirement, offered her frank
opinion and her writing skills, while encouraging
the young, who were lucky enough to have her in
their life.*

*She became my second mother from the moment we
met. Her love extended to my family, which became
hers. I can still see how her eyes lit up when any of
us entered her home.*

*I thank her too for her landscaping talents in what
has become our garden. Each year it gives us a show
with its array of color.*

She is always here.

CONTENTS

I.

"Hope is a memory of the future."

—Gabriel Marcel

road dance

Years ago I killed a cat
flashed on the ramp to the Verrazano Bridge,
crying mouth of the Hudson.

I could not stop in heavy traffic
leaping
doing the twist.

Dance of the streets.

My passenger raised her hand
spoke in Yiddish:
"This cat dies in sacrifice for another.
That is what they said in my lost town
where now only grasses grow."

Years pass.
Today I wear my blue felt hat
with darting feathers and Irish wool
turn up the street and look to the east
in the glare of the just risen sun
a cat is doing the road dance.

White fur glistens pink.
I place the cat to rest on the soft green lawn,
and ask, "For whom did you die?"

daisy chains

The peregrine falcon
swoops down for the catch,
rips off the head.

I did not see the mask on the man
near the side of the road
darkening the sound of your laughter.

Daisy chains link so many generations.

You preen your shiny black-white barred wings
as I search for you.
The moon's downy softness etched a trail
far into the night.
I tried to follow the drift of the stars
round the curve in the road.

So many nights I know not if you are rocked
in the backseat of the car up ahead
or tossed on some grassy slope
by one who stopped to see what else
was connected to your outstretched thumb.

Common burdock clings to worn out cloth
and threads of ancient silk.
You sat and wove a crown of daisies
placed it on my head
said you broke the chain.

I found you singing in the late night café
spilling light.
You scatter petals
rip off the head
fly to your own aerie
black hood
thrust aside.

elephant bone place

Oh Elephant, your smooth sleek skin and eyes
hold remembrance.
I hear you know where to go to die, and the moment
of your transformation.

Join me in keening for your country.
I am with you tonight
as the new moon slices with horns
through the dark sky.

Our culture of greed tears your world,
restless sleepless nights you must spend
seeking the bone place.

I will wear your tusks, shriek out your indignities.
Your eyes so wise, surrounded by wrinkled folds.

Sturdy legs, well grounded, your girth pours into,
gains energy from earth.

I pull your being into my own,
give voice to your retrieval.

Our song trumpets renewal.

sing hallelujah anyway

Moonwashed,
you ran into the night.

I chased you
stopped behind a house lit by fire's glow
in your mountain town.
A woman sat before an old pipe organ
in a goose-down gown
singing: "Hallelujah Anyway".

Snow thick on etched branches
as the moon led me up a long hill
on the side of the road,
crescent the river
wound around like a dark note in a song
melting the frozen snow
waiting to see you.

Back in your house
red handprints on the walls
white powder sifts into shards of brown glass.

I left one who hit me once.
Do you go back for more?

The moon
circle of light
set round you.

Return to the river,
sing "Hallelujah Anyway"
rip it out on the icy snow.

I cross the river to get back on the road,
it wove between us once again.
Had to get lost to find you,
lost to let you go.

II.

"The man who will read no good books has no advantage over the man who can't read them."

—*Mark Twain*

stand down horses

dedicated to Erdine Cathers Antonsen, who lived her truth

When police on horses tried
to break up a demonstration line
Erdine stood with others
in solidarity
not breaking the line.

"I always wondered if I would back down
under pressure," Mother said, pride sparks in her eyes,
"...but I stood up to those horses."

During the challenge concert in 1949,
answer to cross burning snipers roaming the hills,
she stood in the protective ring surrounding Robeson,
so close his sweat glistened,
singing, "Ole Man River".

Aftermath of "Peekskill Riots" foment
a rise of protest when
police stood back, townspeople lined up,
threw rocks at cars stopped at the T
only way out of the concert.
She held the blanket that kept shards
of flying glass from their eyes
driver, a Korean veteran, drove in a crazy zigzag
saved them from harm.

In her last good years she walked
the streets of New Paltz
handed out copies of the *Daily World*,
sent out ten letters to local papers
for their editorial page, said yes I would go through
another heart operation
if I could use the time
to solve the world's literacy problem.

honeysuckle tongue tang

Rain droplet
reflects songster in
moon spangled jeans
dancing.

Rhododendron leaf shelters
timeless time
honeysuckle citrine bursts on tongue
savor midsummer's light
on bone pile reworked.

To mirror is to gift creation's womb
loamy earth
bellflowers
bowing
grace.

Heart song, sing me home.

minnows in milk bottles

Boy and girl
share popping tar bubbles
on summer baked streets
tramp through forests of pines and maples
to swamps collecting cattails to dry
for smoking 'neath the street light's glow

till

his buddies sling darts.

"So long," he says.

"I understand," she lies.

String necklaces with noodles
punctuate with silent question marks,
tramp through fields
search for sassafras and blue periwinkle
lay down, smell salt swamp grass
shut out sun, watch colors through eyelids
catch minnows in milk bottles
let them go

crickets gather in song
take over the silence.

oil slick

Shirley left her landlord's rage and lived with us,
arms circled round black kitten she pulled
from a five-gallon drum of kerosene.

Zeke taught Shirley to fix her car,
charge batteries on our kitchen counter
grind pistons, no mind to the oil slick
tween her breasts.
They got her car purring once again.

Black wad of matted fur kitty rescue
taken from a tar can drowning
nose bubbling plopped in my lap yowling,
settled into a grand purr
forevermore after named Stinky.

Our lives fell apart round then
doctors told mother nervous breakdown
not true—disc slipped
unable to walk to her kitchen.

Shirley added flowers to the center of our table
got us through the day.

Tall agents in trench coats stood across from our
house, watching.

III.

"I refuse to accept the cynical notion that nation after nation must spiral down a militaristic stairway into the hell of nuclear destruction. I believe that unarmed truth and unconditional love will have the final word in reality."

—Martin Luther King

full

Her father forgets to shave often
wears paint-stained overalls
square carpenter's pencil in pocket.

Some folks say he drinks too much.

They live from day to day
in a cyclone of a house
'mongst last week's project
six guppies
soon to be more

and a new experiment

cooked up to show
how oxygen combines with hydrogen
makes water.

He can talk for hours.

She wonders
if there is a question
he can not
answer

so she asks many
and the house
fills up
with more.

capitalism 1952

Our Black Model A Ford sputters and stops.
"This car is just like capitalism," Zeke says,
"always falling apart."

A light bulb shines over his head:
"I'll dress it up for the May Day Parade!
We need something special with McCarthy on watch
and the Rosenbergs sentenced to death."

Shirley paints skulls with vacant eyes staring,
"World Domination or Bust" on the roof.
My mother, Erdine, stirs red food coloring into water.

The day of the march, Eric, Karen and I
ride in the back seat. My sister won't hold my hand,
my brother tells knock-knock jokes.

On Fifth Avenue we pass storefront glitter.
Uncle Sam, my father in top hat and tails at the wheel,
chugs between signs that proclaim:
"Workers of the World Unite,"
 "Free Political Prisoners".

Shirley dressed as a nurse offers marshmallows,
labeled "pabulum for the masses,"
laughing, smiling to the crowd.
Erdine injects inflation with a putty gun into
ballooning tire that pops.

At Union Square the old heap grinds to a halt,
engine overheats. Uncle Sam dismounts
and pours "Worker's Blood" into the radiator,
spews a cloud of steam.

Capitalism dies right there on Union Square.
We all cheer and sing
"Solidarity Forever"
feel united with the world,
the revolution
right around the corner
soon to come.

flare of hope

At ten I know death is a leap into the void—
my dog, Foxy will never come back.
I close my ears to sound
practice blurring my eyes — see
blank spaces where people once stood.

Many come to our door, sit on our porch where
wind chimes tone.
"Best you not know names or faces."
Zeke taps his roll-me-own cigarette.

Spits out one tobacco leaf, eyes locked with mine.
"There are ways they can trick a child."
Is that why he would not let us call him Dad?
Eyes averted, lest I see too much, visitors leave
nameless in the struggle.

Independence Day, 1952

thin Brigadista, from the Abraham Lincoln Brigade
drives up in Chevy delivery truck.
Pulls out a sack of spuds.
"These go back to the Irish famine," he says.
Tucks the eyes into his pocket to replant.

Slices potato meat with ceremony.
Tosses in hot oil, crack and bubble.
We savor taste on tongue with tales of hunger
in the Spanish Civil War,

dark encloses, moon rises.

He packs his flare gun, points to the sky.
"This saved my life when I was lost at sea."
With a bang and pop
flame arcs sky.

Stars wink.

We sing "I dreamed I saw Joe Hill last night,
alive as you and me..."
out of tune, with fervor...
and "Arise, ye prisoners of starvation...
a better world's in birth!"

Mother's eyes shine.

My throat chokes up in anticipation for the day
we'd throw money out the window in bushels.
Value measured each according to their needs.
No one dies of hunger, ever.

challenge

Across the night sky chemical fires burn
green and blue,
Van Gogh splotches streak above the Kill Van Kull
network of creeks dug
to protect the neighborhood lest oil tanks burst.

Father gathers his materials—
metal pipes
rope, cement in burlap,
mound of gritty sand.

Secret smile plays on his lips at his daughter's questions.
Asks her to guess what it would be.
She runs from the orange school bus,
rounding the corner to see the progress.

A frame of pipes etches the sky
rope swings from the top
ready for her to climb
towards her dream of acrobatics in the air.

Ten feet up he says she has twenty more.
Muscles straining,
she nears
her destination.

Surveys the swamps and fields she loves to roam,
the heron pointing towards the Goethals Bridge
a mile away
four maples, leaves turning yellow,
planted by her grandmother years before.

She feels the fibers of the rope,
looks down at his upturned face,
and knows she can reach for more.

IV.

"The brutes and bigots, the batterers and bastards are also children of God(dess).

—Maya Angelou

saturn's return

I brake my racer.
Shirley's house stood here once.

Brambles bite my feet as I lay my bike down.
No sign of imposing dark green hedges,
cut off from the road.

No trace of the foundation.
Tiger lily tangles with Queen Anne's Lace.
Blood spot glitters in the sun.

Shirley sang labor songs, tuned up her car,
wielded a jigsaw to make puzzles for her children—
challenged labels, roles, institutions.

Showed me the world
beneath the surface of the waves.
Flaunted melon breasts, wiggled like Marilyn.
Would feed those babies anywhere, laughed at my scowl
the day she squirted her milk into my face.

My father wanted me to be like her.
She spoke of freedom a lot,
of seagulls swirling in the sky.

Ran home to cook her husband's dinner
kept children quiet
while he chain smoked towards his feet.

I saw the headline:
HUSBAND KILLS WIFE, TOTS, THEN SELF!

No way to read that to reverse the facts.

Lessons come through undercurrents.
Shatter textbook knowledge.
Headlines make reality more real.

The last time I saw her,
aged twenty-nine and I just ten,
my breasts tiny rosebuds.

"Straighten up!" she scolded,
said I hunched my shoulders.
Face red, I watched her speed away
in her black and scarlet roadster,
wishing never to see her again.

And I didn't.

I get on my bicycle.
Turn my back on what has been.
My tires leave no trace.

I look far up the road and speed away.
Wind sleeks my hair, stings my eyes.

My tears flow free.

1·27·01

V.

"We must be willing to let go of the life we planned so as to have the life that is waiting for us.

—Joseph Campbell

light travel at twenty

You call
from a phone booth in the drizzling rain.

Travel light, my young flowers,
so you can move in the middle of the night.
I hold your childhood memories in the attic
so you may come back to where you've been.

The dragon pokes out of a box
while a white-painted unicorn runs round our old town
in a red-paneled truck,
my pastel gown with the long trailing sash
in the very same carton—

I never wore it.

Crimped in the corner
a faded carmine rose....

You stretch through
a picket fence
push past wisteria
for that rose,
pick off all the thorns
before you give it to me.

Travel light—
risk the thorns.

life-saving on location

I pinch my reality with
spiced teas
call back the lilt of your laugh
eyebrows jump up and down
paradox joke supreme
serendipity

sleight of hand
circles at core
positive manipulation
you said
sting

live like you would die
now the only time.

We met atop the co-op, High Falls aerie,
lit a flare to light the night
husband churning up the road at 90mph
whisky by his side.

I could have died that day.

I look for you in the stars.

water bearer

Lightning flashes sky

crystalline rocks stream rain.
Lost, we pass lookalike franchises,
concrete rifts, strip malls and construction—
push and shove steaming
landscape.

Ghosts pull and sway,
whisper of quaint pockets of antiquity

hidden passageway
promenade of palm trees
hotel sprawled out like a three-legged giant,
entry at its center, an old portico.

I carry scraps of paper
to computer
must beat deadline.

Woman in hijab enters to put out
the continental breakfast
works in silence while I search for my words.
Night-time writer I build my own storm—
sheaves of paper fall to the floor—

rush outside to find myself
in moon's sheen
frogs and toads croak and burrow in mud pond
crack of light spills
swallow darts pass on a mission
mockingbird calls.

Quantum energy
awake in early morning mists
I fire off my work
tell the woman we must go.

She rushes behind the curtain,
returns,
offers with gap-toothed smile
two bottles of water
passed like prayers to my waiting hands.

muscadine

Purple loosestrife beckons....
We spread the Army blanket,
mullein pinks crowd to join us.

Sweetflag strays on the far side of the pond,
a merganser follows the others over
cedars pointing....

Bending
you say, "Push them all away, we alone are here."

Tongue flame white heat
red, then
icy blue

I wish to be there with you.

Stick figures peer around gathering clouds,
Father's voice-over reruns
knife in shower
throbs....

slice of hip
meets Camembert,
green grapes....

Your fingers curve
playing, splaying
tongue delta.
You ember my fragments together
smolder bellows within
tongue draw deep the eddy,

smolder licks flame
embers radiating spread
flickering tong....

Lightning etches the moon.

silence speaks
written for Quaker friends married on Summer Solstice

We gather on this Solstice eve
dear friends join in welcome
drink deep the cup of love

as silence speaks.

You who have come so far
converge in a circle of love stone magic.
Let our arms be sanctuary.

I plant sunflowers on the river's path
secret surprise where I know you will pass
over a footbridge
huge sycamore falls into water
branches sip.

The key is under a bluestone near
birdsong and fireflies.
Black sculpted roots
window a scene of your choosing—
perspective is all.
Laurel pink spreads toward mountain tower
myrtle weaves on the edge
spider lights on turbid waters

silent speak breathe.

Sweetflag pokes through
crickets settle in
weaving day into that dark night.

Dear friends together in this moment
we drink from the chalice
as silence speaks:

You who have come so far, so near
converge
join hands across continents in spiral dance.
Earth moves, dancer impels
spirit move,
north running bodies streak light
sanctuary.

the dance

Candlelight flickers
as I glide
into the incense-filled room.

I long to show

you
you

how to fan inner flames
of smoldering desire.

Exalt the freedom
permit ripples
of real feelings to come.

Arms open
zils ringing,

circle
circle

tempt
hints of ecstasy.

Drum gathers momentum.

challenging
challenging

Discover joy
find inner self
unveiled.

VI.

"This we know, the earth does not belong to us, we belong to the earth."

—Chief Seattle

wallkill river powercall

Purple loosestrife
mullein pink gone
willow droops on the water's edge.

Gray skies press brown muddy bank, jagged burr reeds.

I cross iron bridge over the river wishing
to cast aside my fury—
white flame pulse
center
bone cauldron
strong container I chant
petrified past rings red
ancient rhythms stir.

I radiate my rage out
into black rock
past the layers
Paleolithic dream calls
psychic membranes in space.

Hurl whirl orb
into steady waters
tow under
grief
winds gather high
ripple currents

earth breath hearth rhythms cool
streak patterns anew
disengage
let go
heat

draw
rise
fly.

wetland retreat

Waters collect in clouds
fall on mountaintops like prayers——

Floods sluice slopes to the Muhheakantuck,
renamed Hudson on contact
when Europeans touched this soil,
drums echoed earth's tones, maintaining balance.

Sharp leaves spike water pools filtered
through porous karst,
underground tributaries—wetland retreat.

Life brims in transition zone.
Fresh water meets salty sea–estuary, tidal passage.

Otters return, gulls ride the winds.
Dragonflies flying duet shimmer wings,
great blue heron, sentinel in eelgrass
scoops tasty tidbit.

Marsh fosters food chain web.
Blue claw crab and spotted salamander
hide in banks, Arctic seal comes for a visit,
osprey watch above.

Immigrants all—
slog through new territory
now need mending.

Turn to ancient wisdom
save the drowning.

esopus creek watershed tears

Waters wind down
through earth, giant filter to wetlands
for ground water recharge to the Hudson.
Rainbow trout sparkles in Esopus Creek.
Storm floods skim down mountain peaks
spill into Ashokan Reservoir, piped to the city.

Screech of eagle echoes far,
banded raccoon dips morsels in the drink,
deer slips into shadows,
nuzzles dappled fawn in bed of
bloodroot and goldenseal
in a stand of maple.

Belleayre Resort developer tricksters
want to carve up a square mile of wilderness
for condos, hotels, an "organic" golf course—
claim run-off no problem.

Replace ancient forests
block out the stars.

All deserve clear streams.
We are rocks, trees,
whispers
in the breeze.

Coyote tricksters, be on watch.
We see the glow and glitter you seek.
Casino retreat.

VII.

"All real living is meeting."

—Martin Buber

bro

My brother's birthday today.
I finger his number in my hand,
cradle the phone.

Lost at eighteen in skid row, Chicago,
for three months. My mother calls the F.B.I.
figures they tracked us enough—let experts have a try.

They found him
bone thin hobo
atop a cable car,
did not know who he was.

My mother flew to get him.

Our hearts flag those many years
he got caught in the re-vol-ving door
mental units with Thorazine shuffle, shocks,
more meds, alcohol binge, megavitamin rescue reject.

We stood on the scruds
of our remorse, helpless in
obstacle course of psychiatric labyrinths
and did not see our power.

Too, too late
the answer years later comes
a holding tight to the line of love
thrust him into the arms
of his
own
salvage team.

I yearn for his voice.

Only he bellows forth, "Ha…ha-ha,"
in that distinctive way,
echo of my father,
birthday icing on the cake
stance of yesteryear,
sings off key.

I make the call.
hear his laugh,

loud and strong.

dr. ruthless

Master of no thought
going on 'bout
what I should be doin'—
"Stop thinking," you repeat,
"and have you seen your hands in your dream yet?"

You are in my head,
tall woman in black
with kabuki eyes,
brows and smoke puff
synchronize.

We travel together in a pickup truck,
video partners, camp on Superstition Mountain
lamp glowing through desert night.

Coyotes yip.

Meticulous intent matters, you say.
Mountain faces shadow grandeur,
subliminal hues turn
romance rainbow synesthesia.

Coyotes yip.

We pass through
vivid, alive
sentient beings all,
free as your ash meets the sea.

Coyotes yip.

Quarter moon rises.

call witness

Rush through the door where the bamboo
grows wild
round the vine-draped house.

Sharp leaves tap roof
tree frogs call
light candle

hum a lingering tune.
Dance to the muses' agrarian beat,
send and receive hands held tight—

listen for the witness.
Call forward child within
breathe out suffering

find paradox.
Rivers flow,
wind eternally returns.

Take in salt fresh air.
Lush green leaves canopy the porch
greeting one another

amidst spills
of lilacs and honeysuckle,
rain taps elephant ears.

Pen to paper
seeds crack open
words flesh out the page.

Fiery core rises
follow breath
to the altar of joy.

quotidian prayer

Within the walls
prisoners held by bars sit apart
day by day

sharing breathing space.
Despair coats each life
caught in the chains of violence.

Each breath we take has been with us eons
recycled again and again.
Oxygen molecules we breathe today
may have passed through Gandhi's bellows,
Joan of Arc's or maybe those of John Wilkes Booth.

Alternatives to Violence
beams shafts of light
conflict resolution
gifts new ways of reaching out
transforms anger to power within.
Patience and persistence find common ground.

Blind brother in dreads,
feels and hears hearts split open
soft gravelly voice reaches through the cells.

Our breath takes us closer
exhales regrets
inhales forgiveness
day by day.

unstuck heart

Network chiropractor
states spine extension of mind,
muscle clench to ostrich self.
Long-separated body
yearns to drop
armadillo armor.

Says to recall a time
when could not move—
magnify feelings,
live it,
make the sound.

It comes out wail of a trapped seal.

Heart cleaves, holds fast.

Reframe
sound of dolphin sings—
backbone cleaves
release

sense, breath, energy travels new roads,
opens stuck heart
while pride of self fills
strong container, my own bone home,
cauldron of fire.

I feel my body
reap mitochondrial memory
push out of birth canal
new life.

My own gift
I offer.

trust walk

Thunder rolls all day.

In the evening we walk the long path
to the yurt, Turkish domed tent of skins,
step close,
wait for the cosmic shift that brings the peace.

Moon dark night
thunder rolls,
we pass Buddha heads in quiet repose
on fallen logs, rising through the trees.

Vines tangle in the forest,
we read our work.
Coyotes yip. A long wail splits the night—
screams of a predator's prey reaches our ears

halts our words.

Water, then, spills from the sky,
rushing away the hot, steamy night—
tropical downpour.
Open spoken
we shout through the flow.
tongues wrapped 'round words,
spit them out to the night
where they whip around unleashed.

We come out between the storms.
Fireflies dance,
Van Gogh splotches in the dark canvas sky.
Mountain dark meets night blue
heat lightning strobes the way.

waterfall meet-up

My body weeps
long held tears flow.

Energy workers
in yoga, scents and candles
spread crystal visions—
Somato-psychic waves
bring back feeling.

Quantum leaps—

I seek
strains of DNA,
between dimensions.
Vision a waterfall meet-up.
Falls roar, sheer power tumble misty cloud,
flowing water curtain parts
huge rock cliff our stage.

Spirit enters, long gown with corset and bustle
gazes at my floppy hat and jeans, lips purse.
We ask together, "How can you breathe?"

I see a roll of her eyes,
that certain tilt of chin I've seen before.

We stay up all night,
laugh and dance on the strobes.

VIII.

"Joy upon joy and gain upon gain are the destined rights of my birth. And I shout my praise of my endless days to the echoing edge of the earth."

—Jack London

off the grid

Trucks packed
computers
notepads,
modern Conestoga
retrace ancestor's path
travel to build homestead
in view of the Spanish Peaks, Wahatoya,
earth's breast
wild never tamed.

Seeds started
gal in work boots, long hair and sunglasses,
holds pit bull in lap grinning tongue drips
happy.

Guy driving Blazer shares their smile
mad scientist
engineer ready for new climate
enterprise
architects change.

Leave Asphalt State
for critter project
blog adventures
make power
sun and wind,
earth and its fire
get off the grid.

Build refuge,
gardens zen
brick ovens.

They rush,
to bond with Yonkers the Yak, mom-to-be,
before baby Yeti is born,
or she may attack with horns.
Teach sister Yazoo to give milk for cheese.

All laughs playing with Y names
spinning words and silk hair.

Battered but tough pickup driver follows,
scared but anticipating
growing loofah gourds
in hydroponic tubs.

We warm our hands by their fire.

ulster manor retro

I am here to speak for the waters who
cannot speak for themselves.

In a wetland near the Hudson
a bog turtle struggles through
phosphorus spawned algae plumes.

Vernal pool drained
hungry fish swim to deeper waters
salamander can lay eggs in peace.

Archeological treasures
slated for dismemberment to make
landscaped housing tracts
profiteers cover up reports to the planning board
for easy pass.

In a verdant forest where archeologists found
Esopus Munsee burial sites
lithic workshop fine points
crafted four thousand years ago
stocked atop rougher cuts of flint.

We call our tribes together to sing our sacred songs
save this ridge for children
seven generations hence, in the shelter of white pine,

their minds growing strong.

clarion

Rooster crows.
Must be crazy, I think,
cloud slips away, showcasing the moon

witness.

Peacock's primal cry splices dreamtime
coo of mourning dove
lulls me back

breath
energy
push away the nay—
past, past, past.

Connect wisdom
in my own bone home
cauldron solid, protected.

Dance and ride inner canoe
candles float across sylvan lake
alter self waves
Mandarin breeze
joy moves in.

Presence
on-call animus
show up for life.

ACKNOWLEDGEMENTS

I offer gratitude to my husband, Bill Brown, co-owner of Brillig's Books, who helps me put my writing on the top of the list, and shares my life with joy. Each morning we give thanks for one another.

I am grateful to my heroine, Colleen Geraghty, who insisted I meet Catharine Clarke, my writing coach, editor, and now publisher. And gratitude also goes to Jody Abbott whose breathtaking artwork made the beautiful cover of this book and enchanced its contents. Thanks to those who gave nods of encouragement from a young age. To Diane Bonner, bibliotherapist, for always being there for the word; Diane Eichelberger, who chews those words making great patterns of sound, and Denis Scanlon, who writes pictures in verse, and challenges me to make him see what I write. To Maayana Howard with a great ear and Marc Rabinowitz, Network chiropractor extraordinaire.

To Fred Harris and Toni Horvatin teachers of "Spontaneous Theatre," often first audience to my stories. To Pat Clarke at the SUNY New Paltz Women's Studies Program and Gale McGovern, for early guidance. To my friends, Jody Abbott, Johanna Hill, Elaine Kniffen, Phyllis Rosner, Fred

Steuding, Marian Tortorella, all early ears for my work. To my dear sister, Karen Cathers, who surprises me with her version of the same story; her partner, Miriam Strouse, and to my brother, Eric Antonsen, sometimes muse. To Pat Tucci, writing mentor, and Joni Miller of Open Spoken for her support and critiques. To Nathan Koenig and Shelli Lipton for their outstanding work as founders of the Woodstock Museum, Saugerties. To Jude Andreasen, Robin Birdfeather, Lynne Holstein, Nancy Headapohl, Jan Koehler, Sandi Miller, Cleve Overton, Rainbow Weaver, and Harry Wirtz, and my ongoing healthy foods and writing group members: Karen Cathers, Helen Fogarty, and Esther Frances. To WBAI-FM for my sanity and Family Runaway House in Woodstock, New York for their invaluable support.

My special appreciation also goes to Jay Blotcher, Roberta Gould, Gary Irving, and Laura Drew Kelly for their generous words in support of this book.

Thanks to my daughter, Halina Adamski, who helps me as editor and critic; to my son André Adamski, for his ancestral studies and independent fire, and to my daughter, Janette Hansen, for teaching me with her growth. To Cyndi Gawronski and Sandra Oxford who became my daughters the easy way. To my grandchildren and great-grandchildren, nieces, nephews, and cousins, gifting their mix of reality soup. Cheers to friends who smiled on hearing I was still writing away.

In memoriam to: Dominic Chiapperino, my fifth grade teacher, who challenged me to write a play, to find my voice; to my father, Zekor Antonsen, who became my first writing collaborator; to my mother, Erdine Cathers Antonsen, who taught me the meaning of love; to Carley Bogarad, dedicated teacher at SUNY New Paltz; Betty Cheyne, video partner, and Phil Rosner and Ingrid Shepard, wise friends.

gracias
mitaquye oyashin
namaste

ABOUT THE AUTHOR:

Elga Antonsen is the daughter of the only open Communists in Staten Island during the McCarthy era, Erdine, a school teacher and literacy advocate and Zeke, a carpenter, mad scientist and philosopher. She started out life with the unique perspectives and challenges grown from that time. Originally planning to become a veterinarian or scientist, Antonsen instead managed to raise three children, while working on her writing. Her published work includes *Daring to Dream*, New Era Publishers, New York, 1977. Residing in Kingston, New York, she is co-owner of Brillig's Books, an antiquarian online bookstore with her husband, Bill, and has served in AVP, the Alternatives to Violence program. With several works of fiction on the burner, she and her sister are presently collaborating on a novel about their experiences.

Her collection of poems, **road dance**, can be ordered online via Amazon or Barnes and Noble or directly from the author at: www.brilligsbooks@brilligsbooks.com

ABOUT THE ARTIST:

"As in primary cultures, my art is an integral part of my life, abandoning the traditional precepts and techniques in which I was trained, I seek to perceive and convey a sense of the unique spirit of a place. Working on location allows me the sublime experience of being part of a sacred space, one in which I belong."

—Jody Abbot lives and paints in the Catskill Mountains of New York

LaVergne, TN USA
30 June 2010
187894LV00001B/4/P